EASY FIX

EASY FIX

Blair Trewartha

Palimpsest Press
1171 Eastlawn Ave.
Windsor, Ontario. N8S 3J1
www.palimpsestpress.ca

Book and cover design by Dawn Kresan. Typeset in Optima and
Adobe Garamond Pro, and printed offset on Rolland Zephyr Laid at
Coach House Printing in Ontario, Canada. Edited by Jim Johnstone.

Palimpsest Press would like to thank the Canada Council for the Arts,
and the Ontario Arts Council for their support of our publishing
program. We also acknowledge the assistance of the Government of
Ontario through the Ontario Book Publishing Tax Credit.

Library and Archives Canada Cataloguing in Publication

Trewartha, Blair, 1983–, author
Easy fix / Blair Trewartha.

Poems. ISBN 978-1-926794-22-8 (pbk.)

    I. Title.

PS8639.R483E28 2014   C811'.6   C2014-902107-0

for Erika

Contents

PROCEDURES FOR ESCAPE

PORCUPINE, BURNING

THE DARKEST DAY OF THE YEAR

PROCEDURES FOR ESCAPE

Time Lapse of a City

Across the city someone wraps
a lit apartment around their shoulders,
reads a book until
the last word is *sleep*.

A doctor grips the steering wheel,
pulls a scalpel from beneath the seat
and prays for the next red light,
a sudden traffic jam.

An engineer spreads his wings
and jumps. Telemarketers still
dial their Mothers' numbers
at the start of every shift.

Somewhere a man forgets
his address at Starbucks
and sits for hours, body
pressed up to the window
until he's baptized.

Somewhere loud music hits
and the city becomes a flock of pigeons,
cooing. An entire world
with its ducks
in a row. Feathers brushing
against feathers for warmth.

Undertaking

—For Zoey

This is sacred ground.

At the Parlor, there's a 20 year old
drained of blood,
a woman working his hands—
nails trenched through elastic neck,
flesh wounds of reflexive regret.

On dates, she tells men
what she does for money,
decides to take them home
when they compare her
to a doctor.

Alone, body sprawled stiff,
she kneads knots from muscle,
tension from bone—

always push and pull,
savor and withdraw—
something like a baker
or backwards God.

Counting House

Month. Day. Year. Like counting
the bobbing heads of school kids
on a bus, or the nickel and dime
jumps of the rotating taxi dash.
You've never felt this way,
like the whole world is a lamp-
shade. I'll bet you were bathed
in fluorescents all your life,
sun roof on your car, a sky
light in your cubicle. I've been
making airplanes out of wedding
invitations and birthday cards.
Promising to send gifts
then forgetting to forget.
Watching calendar days pass
like commercials, a message
loading itself, eventually.
There's no place like home
in the corner of an amphitheater.
No medicine like laughter
from the outside in. If I stepped
off a bus and got struck by lightning,
I could finally smoke a cigarette
and beat the odds. Double down
on everything except you.
I could take your hand and check
your sleeves, but you'd just wave
them like the queen.
And I'd be left alone, counting.

Procedures for Escape

The train hovers along the track
between Oshawa and Belleville
and I sit in seat 14
in the aisle across from the emergency window
with a little red hammer
in a small gray box—
the one which every kid, including me
would give up their seat
just to smash

The attendant explains the procedures of escape
to the family of five sitting ahead of me
She's a cute brunette with high cheekbones
and low lips and probably close to my age
and she asks me if in the event of an emergency
would I be willing to climb out the window with her first
and help her assist all the women and children off the train

I tell her yes, and stare back out the window
at the blurred trees and old telephone wires
listening to the sounds the train wheels make
across the rails
which always sound a bit like thunder
or a steel mill in full work-day swing
and I imagine the two of us, hand in hand
leaping out the shattered window
looking like two children jumping off a small cliff
into blue water on a sun-blind afternoon
using our fear of heights
as a meager excuse to hold hands

I look back at the tiny red hammer
in the little gray box
displayed like a javelin
and repeat her question over again in my head
thinking, yes I'm willing to do that
you're just the first person
to have asked

Planet B

For the first time, an earth-sized planet
has been found in the hospitable zone.
A small red dwarf star cooler than our sun.

Thousands of people list their apartments
or homes. From mo-town to grow-town,
investors flock to fine art, great directors

and the movies they never made.
A part-time pooch. A kitchen library.
Ontario kids find weird, shiny objects

while digging for worms. Keep calm,
we're all trying to figure out how to navigate.
Lightening looking for answers,

a hanging halted by the victim's mom.
This is a tour of the animal kingdom
as you've never seen it before: a detachable,

swimming penis; violent bedbug sex.
My little baby is in the sea.
Oprah, please return this woman's calls.

We are not dead yet. There is no planet B.

Moving Days

This afternoon will leave
us tired, negotiating

transit maps
and picking pockets.

A man purchases a parking permit
while brushing his teeth.

A woman hangs drapes
in a bus shelter,

calls everyone she knows
in for tea.

It should be different,
less venom, more heart.

An easier place to rest
when our legs ache.

Instead,
strangers puff up

chests, and the doors we knock
on open like accordions.

On Waking on a Mortgage Broker's Lawn

Subway stations,
after hour clinics,
all upholstered
like an English
rain cloud—
places we enter,
then feign
control. Once,
at dawn, I woke
in a strange city
on a mortgage
broker's lawn.
A friend lying
next to me nodded
and we looked
through
a flash in a tunnel,
the pigeonholed
circus of a nurse's
ball-point pen.
They come at us
like a Dart
charging the highway,
bucking every
object in its path.

Going On

I singled them out. Ordered them
to stand up and film me, falling.

Told them if they couldn't name it,
if we couldn't stretch

and slap our limbs against the wall,
then we'd all lose.

My ex with a twist in her hair,
my brother yelling over and over

as my wife stepped closer to wrap
my wrists until they bled

into the backs of my shoes. Asked
if I needed another beer.

Perhaps it was a party all along?
A party I left, that went on.

Matachika

Money flutters through the lobby
like a damaged bird.

Matachika—an island
that launders culture,
      caters to husbands barking
over lost cabana keys,
      locals chasing wind-swept

chairs. Spanish slurs
through walkie talkies—
      tourists drop their drinks,
      ignore the woman scraping
glass with her hands.

Later, clouds curl,
      double over with surf
blowing from behind,
      the credit machine
gleaming—

and our leashed retriever
flails,
      body flopping in sand,
      as he tries to sprint
towards the shore.

Determinism

We were nothing more than dominoes
beating and beating and beating
until the fall. You were cruel,
yet still I'd wait on those steps—
feel the bricks dislodging,
shutters slapping windowpanes.

Cracks in the sidewalk
recall a million times I broke our Mother's back—
face bursting across cement,
your hand on the back of my head,
laughing: *You did it! You landed on the lines!*
Trapping me until the door opens.

Afraid of closed rooms,
I enter like a nurse. Distrust
anyone at dawn. Home a tire swing
you flung from daily, a thing learned
once that held us forever. We should
have named it before it was gone.

Passives

Hesitant hiss,
a muffled puff of flame,
        the hairs sprouting
                from your knuckles, singed.

Inaudible fuck
        suspended between throat and palate—
                hand cooling beneath a tap.

It's dangerous
this suppression of reflex,
        things we should have said
                but didn't—
                        patterns imprinted on the brain.

And it will end this way—
syllables unvoiced,
        contraction of flesh and tongue,
                a pain you try to ignore.

A Mortician Considers Formula One

Imagine breasts amidst the flowers.
The horsepower behind a pipe organ
playing mourners to their seats.
We'd all sleep a little better, wouldn't we?
Burials just midnight burn-outs
down boulevards and beach front,
flames splashing across a hearse.

Imagine my bicep across the jumbo-tron,
pulling the driver from his satin
pillow through a crumpled door.
An audience of chins dropping
in prayer. Then the final curtain:
he's aaaaallright folks ... the collective
relief. A different type of *Amen*.

Until Paralysis

—For K.B.

At night her son is all white
heat and jaw
strength until paralysis.

She screams in English
because that's what comes out,
her fear external,

a slur of medical acronyms
like a robe thrown
on for cover. Days later his face

tattooed beneath the eyelid
with each flinch, every tilt
of the head. On skype she lies

to her Mother in Nepalese:
translation of *we're all fine*—
hand on the scruff of his neck,

the sequenced tapping of a cell phone.

Before Leaving for Sudbury

Down the highway I see you
holding kettle bells,
your head turning, not knowing
where to put them down.

I should have shoved you
off a cliff. Snapped your legs
over a turnstile. Instead,
my departure has become

a passport—the way your lips
tremble and curl, swell
with sound. When I finally
reach Sudbury, the muscles

in my back contract, tiny blown
fuses along my spine. Here's
a ticket no one will ever check.
It gets you out of anywhere.

Civic Elegy

In the winter, tire tracks in snow.
Morning Radio. The feeling
that every family Christmas
is at least one type of funeral.

I'm afraid these ribbons
will only hold so long
before someone pushes through.

I'm afraid of the bathroom
light-flick rush of centipedes—

in the heat of August, the quarry
I used to jump from,
but only the platform,
that space and time my feet

were still flat on the rock:
bone dry, dead weight.

I'm afraid to look at the clothesline
at night, of going blind a third time.
I'm afraid of being my father,
the edge of a building but not the fall,

that gut feeling every time
I meet someone new,
the noose-pull of a social greeting.

PORCUPINE, BURNING

Honeymoon

Fortune hunters hurdle over eskers and muskeg.
Grub stakers fake their claim, trip up city slickers
on pillow lava and painted quartz, lose them through
a solid wall of jack pines.

We thread veins into the forearm of the Porcupine.
If ever we see gold, we are surgeons
etching yellow from red, shovels and pick axes
scalping out the cancer from the flesh.

I trip in the dirt and look up, breathless.
A golden staircase ripples down a cliff face.
We grab shotguns and set up camp. Protect our plot
like a wedding vow for an entire month.

Porcupine, Burning

July 11, 1911

I wake hung over. Head a sponge wrenched dry.
Bile gurgling in the belly and wood smoke burning nose hairs
like miniature wicks. An instant, jerking cough.
Outside birch ash spreads across a cloudless sky. Trees roar.
Consume themselves. Lay limbs across the backs of prospectors,
caress them with the warmth of a mother as their bodies ignite,
hands still searching for gold.

> Fire is a thing we want to enter, a chimera, a brick wall
> without a solid grasp or liquid to run our fingers through.

Paint begins to bubble on the courthouse at the edge of town.
Windows sweat and char in saloons. Untying horses, I strip naked,
dunk my clothes in the well before putting them on again.
When the first row of houses collapses, horses are panicking
in the water. Hides leathered. In a mirage of steaming denim,
I watch townspeople swarm to the lake with billfolds and jewelry
in their arms. Crawling and sputtering the last few yards
until they nosedive beneath the surface—coats splayed
open like parachutes.

> It's the recovery we fear most, the weight of metal
> and that first scratch of dirt. We try to bend
> ourselves to weather.

> Rely on ore, copper. Hold sun in rock form, sweat
> evaporating on our hands.

Those of us who make it float in the harbour,
cup our collars over our mouths. The fields swell
with rabbits and deer, the odd black bear.
We tread and watch the drowned transform.
They become wall-eyed. Grow fins on the backs of their arms.
Scales shimmering off the surface as they shed their flesh
and clothes. We turn our chins upward to the sky
where smoke forms puddles that birds dive into—tiny beaks
of gold plummeting, tails trailing like kites.

Retrieval

A St. Bernard coddles her pups. Five sets of paws curled over a floating
fence post—one hundred feet of flames quivering behind. Each time one
slips beneath the surface, she tugs at the scruff of its neck, pulls its body
onto the preserver—and I wake. Reach for your arm. Finger your
hair. I never told anyone I found you, sleeping in the charcoal
of our house. They'd take you to the river in burlap, mark you
with dynamite crates and a charred canoe. So at night I protect
you from bears. Throw stones at bobcats. Train my rifle on the wolves
around the dumpsite, ready to pull if they veer off-track. Holding your
hands in my armpits to warm you.

> When one mind falters another snaps loose. Focuses a sunspot
> where blood lies, silver where grey flesh lays in soil.

> The weaker mind burrows itself under rock, folds the other
> over its vertebrae. A fossil inside a cocoon, gushing
> water encased in a shell of layered ice.

An explosion of seagulls in the field and it's morning. I leave you
sleeping in the tent and grab my pick axe. Join the others near the drills.
Help children peel up moss. Weigh each drop of gold burned
into the shield like candle wax. At day end we count the pounds
together, calculate the weight in dollars, monthly wages, a house.
Fire a backhanded blessing—to have cleared months of tree cutting
in a single night. I rub your fingers before we sleep. I do everything
I can to make you warm.

Vigil

"Find the few living things
rotting fast in their sleep of the dead"
—Sufjan Stevens

The wagons are rolling to Golgotha.
Atop, the dead sit upright,
holding the heads of the living.
A bend in the road and wooden planks
beneath their bones turn like a carousel,
a little battle of blackened femurs
and hollowed skulls, dancing in unison.
When the sun hits, just right,
adipose comes pouring back. Infused,
they revert to chubby miners giggling
on a wagon ride. But when the clouds
eclipse, I see ivory again. Lenses
without shutters, flayed men carted
to the woods, a flutter of severed strings.
Calcified, the cargo folds like kindling.
Once they saw fortune in chunks of rock,
amateur alchemists experimenting
in beds of lichen, clenching fists of cash.
Now, we landscape. Erect tents in old plots,
angled for success. In the snuffed
out match head of our town,
each heave of carcass is a transaction.

Recovery

"And knowing how the common-folk condemn
what it is I do, to you, to keep you warm"
—Joanna Newsom

The doctor won't look at you. I told him you're sick,
but he keeps shaking his head, cups my shoulder with his hand.
When he swallows I see his throat bubble, pockets of air
morphing like cauliflower. He coughs and the ground shakes.

We haven't held a card game since the fire. Keep telling me they need to
get some sleep. Everyone is acting strange. The children throw pebbles,
paint dung for me to discover, kick me as I bend to retrieve
them. When I lunge forward, my eyes are mason jars full of fireflies.

I collect yellow dust and tiny pebbles from boot
collars and coveralls when day shift ends, duck my head at the broom
swing of a foreman, and bury them near our camp.

When you're well enough, I'll retrieve them, sell our entire plunder
in town and head back south. This could be the only escape we have left.
Fleeing in a cloud of seagulls, a herd of collared miners massaging
their backs.

But for tonight, I pilfer the blown-out railway. Pocket shafts of iron
too bent to reuse. These will be my weapons at night. The things I'll hurl
in darkness at sounds of predators—the weight that keeps my torso
pinned beside you on the ground.

Breaker

In the lake, I am heavy. I am stone.
Gravity releasing its grip

until I roll effortlessly, vertebrae separating,
spine snapping into alignment.

I used to call you a bitch when we'd fight.
Your slick skin maneuvering through the reeds

like a ghost, jagged rows of teeth
hidden beneath the bed sheet.

Even your bite I miss, that sudden punch of breath
at the moment of puncture. The injection of pulse.

Anything is better than this—a stillness more solid
than shore. Your silence an undertow I waltz with blindly.

Pallbearers

At night, men came for you. I lay twisted in a puddle of urine, smelled of kerosene and copper, paralyzed in a bed of bent rails. They looked up for me, once. A shotgun turned like a periscope in the dark. Then one by one they lifted your body, tugged at each limb, nearly plucked one from the socket. The youngest threw up and dropped you, covered you with burlap. The eldest grabbed up the slack, pulled it above your head and tied a knot. A sac of grain strong-armed in a mill yard, a pallbearers' procession of men who taunt me. I imagined you thrashing, head thrown back, jaw wrenched in a scream. A knot unfurled, a foot torn loose from a clasped fist, and my legs would pump with adrenaline. I'd break free and barrel toward you—they'd never see me coming. A bull trampling an entourage of armed men. The piss soaked derelict running to save his wife.

Severed

I

I open my eyes in the scrap yard without you.

I hear children prattling about the coming Magician,
the inch count of saw blades, the bulbous heft
of the assistant's breasts—how he'll cut her right in half.

II

Most of us never made it, or tripped up half way,
found later bent over canoe lips, legs waterlogged,
backs seared and desiccated.

Two months later, it's a crop of drug stores and insurance
brokers, bloodlet soldered into footprints
on a boardwalk made of imported pine.

Where the explosives sat before, a fresh spring now lies,
suckled by throat-dry deer and teenagers
doing belly flops, spiraling air-bound as they flex their abs.

III

Before the fire, Porcupine was a powder keg of progress,
an entire crate of dynamite planted in the ground.
Then, a single reaching flame

and with the flick of its tail, the brush of a wooden leg—
there's a pond blown-out like a plucked eye socket.
We swim within it, seeing nothing.

Lay claim to severed bush plots. Write letters down south
recruiting newlyweds and distant cousins,
their starched shirts getting swept up in the rush.

Vaudeville

Nothing cuts like amber. This shard, it slivers
its way into skin, then disappears.
I use it to carve into the neck of a birch,
our names gouged like boot prints through snow.
In town, they celebrate. Drunken kings
in a courtyard of toy thrones. The Magician
peels back the tablecloth, parades his assistant
in a corset of hip turns and twitching
calf muscles.

This is the magic. How one woman can
herd and collar an entire town of brutes
twice her size. Snapping fingers
with powder bombs of talcum, rotations
of solid oak and the glint of blades,
the blood test of a calloused thumb.
The town lingering on the anticipation
of an impaled breast.
The corset a blindfold for a darker lust.

As the first plunge of the blade—a guttural
echo, then a plume of whiskey
in a cloud of laughter. I see tendons
severing, blood seeping through fatty tissue
like oil hemorrhaging in fields.

The second thrust slashes a web of nerves.
Even in slaughter she smiles, perfectly,
her turtle-shelled body
rotating on a pivot, a flip book of entry
and exit wounds. And it's this peace I need,
the euphoria of dissection. I want to know how
it feels to be put back together as the whole
town applauds—women tearing up,
everyone smiling, drinking to survival.

Parting

I wait for an avalanche. A mountain's chest
to come pummeling down and unearth me.

I want to be gutted like a sow on a string,
window-framed and hanging.

You were going to be gorgeous.
I was going to be strong.

Now I carry your torso like a chain that can't be unhooked,
my mind a series of sparks waiting to be lit.

This heat is a tree I'd like to climb, barefoot,
breaking through the surface until there's only sky.

I wander through a sea of tents—
children run beside me collecting silver droplets in a cup.

I am a goat splayed open under moon.
Timber burning forever.

I collapse beneath cloud cover on a sundial.
Everyone else is warm.

THE DARKEST DAY OF THE YEAR

The Darkest Day of the Year

For a split second, the snow
is a glacial overhang,
a frozen levy ready to melt
the moment I step indoors.

I picture myself swinging
from a web of hydro wires
in a snowsuit: crashing
through windows and slapping

husbands, kissing their wives.
Lighting my blowtorch
in their bedrooms to bring spring.
Everyone cheering for the man on fire.

Easy Fix

Large nets hang from the ceiling,
palms table-topping your lungs.

A single grain pinched between
fingertips. Your bed a weigh scale—

ready to drop.

We know you from the water that rolls
off you in the rain.

Now, you smell of kerosene.
A thin wheeze with every breath.

This could be an easy fix,
if only you'd just lie down.

We would all gather around, watching.

Pluck that first string with a pocketknife.
Crack open a window to let in some air.

Liminal

In the abandoned farmhouse we watch.
The sagging backdrop, rotting porch.
The lump of overgrown grass where
my father buried the dog. I rehearse,
avoid eye contact with the cement slab
where my grandfather shot cattle,
the cemetery at the edge of the property
line. I imagine our coach dying
inside a bulldozer, caught on a bridge
in an ice storm—transport swerving,
the spark at impact. Rain pelted
the windshield, his son forever terrified
of storms. Two years later, Angie
was struck by a car—a weight that
changed form instantly. We visited her,
drunk at 2am, stared at plastic flowers,
the sketch of birds and meadows burned
into black stone. When I propose
to my wife in the fallow field,
we announce ourselves—stand above
our grandparents' and uncles' graves,
flash the ring, whisper one another's names.

Animus

I. *Erwin, Tennessee*

Backstage, beasts trample
paths between tarp walls
and tiki torches—audience
awed by trapeze artists
and men who place their heads
in the mouths of lions.

Bull hook glistening, a trainer
prods Mary the elephant's
ear and her grey grip
of muscle rages, wraps
around his waist and heaves
him into the barn wall.

The citizens call for her head.
They gather at the railway
gallows, watch her hang
from a crane, vertebrae
splintering—thick
trees folding through storms.

II. *Long Clawson, England*

We are feeble without firearms,
hands hogtied in red tape
from office desk drawers,
rows of twelfth century vicars
and clergymen exhumed by the teeth
of burrowing carnivores.

At dawn, the groundskeeper scours
the graveyard on bone patrol,
collects fibulas and clavicles
in a rusty wheelbarrow, and re-inters
them before the neighborhood children
wake to walk their dogs.

III. *Campbellton, New Brunswick*

Packaged like cigarettes on the floor
of an above-store apartment,
their schoolboy bed-heads tussle out
of shirt collars like loose
flakes of tobacco.

Below, smoke slides through
heating vents, bombs the wall—
when it reaches them,
they'll forget to breathe.
Or scream.

Feel its weight, the oxygen
pulled from their lungs.
Hear the sudden hiss
as someone inhales, deeply.

Then the crushing bear hug
of half-sleep, a midnight check-in
after the babysitter goes home,
or the kids come back
from a slumber party.

IV. *Saskatchewan*

In Saskatchewan, a storm is brewing. Cattle huddle beneath a tree in the rain; a hundred snakes skim the hallways of a hospital.

                       Lights out and a woman thrusts a broom handle at wings beating against the hammock of a light fixture. Bats entangle like stems in a bouquet of flowers as she sleeps.

With just a single flash, the entire herd of cattle is laid out—eighteen giant bellies sinking into the soil.

Rollover

You remember the cicada's siren,
reeds bent beneath a boot,
snapped in half. Then an echo
like screaming into a tin can.

Frog cradled in hand, legs a pair
of crooked Ls trying to leap.
You remember clinging to a tree.
Herpetologists pulling the sheets

back to find an empty gurney—
a lily-pad of melted skin.
They interrogate you now:
"Where are you from? What happened after?"

But you're just cold and need water.
Body pulsing. Ready to jump.

Lighting up Dark Valleys
—after Martin Anderson

Next time the world opens up beside you,
everyone will be there;

the skeptics, the haters and lovers alike
gathered in the square the day it brightens.

I'll stand back with a martini, watching.
Weeks before, the helicopters hovered,

dangling plates of glass like three giant
diamonds hung between a pair of breasts.

Everyone said it shone like a spotlight,
the stage a square of cobblestone,

audience dumbstruck by the engineering,
the art of it all. Someone, somewhere

actually quoted Joshua 10:13. Even
the town historian was trickled into his seat

to inhale, darkness already a memory,
a time of century-old cable cars strung up

the mountainside, the daily delivery of sun-
starved workers to the solar patch at the peak.

You all called me stupid, and now you feed
from the cup. To me, if I'm honest,

it's all reminiscent of a mirrored
backdrop to snow-topped ridges, white light,

the instant draw, that ability to see so
much more than nature provides.

Noon, glaring, not yet gone to bed.
The darkness just around the edges.

Cut and Dry

I mounted you on your way
out the door, poured my hands
over you like a showerhead,
like I had something to prove.

Later, we dried off with
damp towels and dirty t-shirts.
You left for your meeting
smelling like both of us.

Out on the back porch,
I sit beneath a clothesline
full of white dress shirts
drying in the dark.

Break In

—On Ernest Shackleton's Voyage

Their hearts beat
despite three days
without food,
four days
paddling through snow.

On elephant island
one man, crazed,
wields an axe,
plunging it into blubber—

blood sprays across snow
heads pluck off seals
and twenty more corpses
flop through
the frigid surf
marking
the swift entrance
of man.

Electric Fence

The phone rings—
we bake in the heat
of small town verandas,
Grandmother's pickles
cooling our tongues.

She drops it—
arms clutching my Uncle's
waist as he reaches
for the falling receiver,
fingers tangled
in curled white chords
like a mountain climber
clinging to rope.

We answer innocuously.
Syllables connecting,
climbing onto our lips
to wait, to un-deliver a loved.
Moments we plug in lamps,
before they light every inch
of the room.

Soon I stumble across a dead cow
in the barnyard, float back
from its sprawled tongue,
flies circling inner eyelids
and the dried cavern of its nose—

reeling all the way
into the electric fence,
my body suspended
in a seizure of kilowatts,
tears pooling
like light.

Fungus Gnats and Facial Hair

Tonight I spray the houseplants
for fungus gnats
until wings glue to backs
and bodies lay motionless,
drowned

Larva embed in soil,
twist and writhe into death
as thinly curled hairs
fall black from my chin
like leaves

I brush my teeth,
contemplate the intricacies of growth,
facial hair and insecticide—
flies swarming my bedside,
flightless and bald

Coming Down

Blood-red alarm clock numbers
flash the size of transport brakes,
the furnace hums

My forehead burns—
t-shirt drenched through to sheets,
leaving me shivering
in the paradox
of breaking fever

It's almost painless.
She gathers the most fragile parts of me
in the hopes I'll sleep
before delirium

In the morning I wake
calved from whatever beast
held me—

skin tepid as pond water,
sober and cold

3 days in a Korean Hospital

and my optic nerve
swells like the worms
of rotten potatoes
we call eyes

Tongueless stranger,
symptoms aphonic,
speech seeps
into walls and windows
the way mold pulls colour
from spoiled fruit

Voices bend
behind curtains and gurneys,
flustered nurses
mutter in Hangul,
shot-gun prednisone—

a smile of sorts
sweeps across my face

Breaking Points

I used to pray incessantly.
Not to god, but to prevent
the sway of sucker
punches, the flash of red
and echo of every elevator.

I used to pray for shadow,
someone larger standing behind me.
To not be peeled back
like a jacket
exposing the tangle
of kites strung to my chest.

How do I tell my old friend
I'm scared of him now?
And cocaine. Or just that I'm thirty,
and no longer live my life
like a bed spring. How do I decide *this*
is what I'm going to do, or not do,
for the rest of my life?

When I love something
I hold it like a grudge.
Pray that loved ones won't die
on nights I'm left alone,
then daydream they do.
I wash the dishes over and over again;
let them dry on some
newspapers on the floor.

This is how simple it could be:
a little patch of cloud in a clear
blue sky. The mix of water and trees.
Instead, the nights are black
moments of dead air.
Knots turning my knuckles blue.

Palaver

There's space here, at night.
There's a separation you could
slide your entire body through.
We have to call this something.

We wake in the morning
with arms full, lungs opening
into winter, inhaling the burden
of bent bows.

You sleep curled into the headboard.
I roam the highway, remembering
how it grows—how it dies
without a body to be anchored by.

Final Credits

Remember it all but picture
this: a white screen

to replace the windows,
an all encompassing

focal point—heads tilted
forward like a mass

of flagpoles blowing in
the wind. We are

the generation that disregards.
We wake tethered,

thin cement in our veins,
fish-facing the glass.

Language just a string
of broken dollar signs

twisted at the ends. When
we're dug up centuries

from now, they'll scribble
a warning: contents

may fall apart, or explode.
Handle with care.

Notes

'Planet B' is a found poem, constructed from a series of random, disconnected headlines from various news websites, including the CBC, CNN, *Toronto Star*, and *Huffington Post*.

The last line of 'Going On' was inspired by Ken Babstock's 'Materialist' in *Airstream Land Yacht* (House of Anansi, 2006).

The 'Porcupine, Burning' suite is a fictional narrative based on The Great Porcupine Fire of 1911, in which the Northern Ontario mining town burned to the ground in a massive forest fire.

'Animus' is a suite of poems inspired by real life interactions between animals and humans from various time periods, including both historical and present-day events.

'Lighting Up Dark Valleys' is a fictional narrative from the perspective of Martin Anderson, the artist behind the use of giant mirrors to light the valleys of the Norwegian town of Rjukan, which goes without direct sunlight for half the year.

'Break In' is based on the voyages of Ernest Shackleton and his crew aboard the Endurance, particularly the moment they first landed on Elephant Island.

Acknowledgments

Some of the poems in *Easy Fix* previously appeared in *Canadian Literature, Contemporary Verse 2, ditch, Existere, Misunderstandings Magazine*, and *Prism International*. They also appeared in the limited edition chapbooks *Break In* (Cactus Press, 2010) and *Porcupine Burning* (Baseline Press, 2012). Thanks to the editors of each.

A heartfelt thank you to the writers and editors who supported me throughout the creation of this book: Julie Cameron Gray, Sam Cheuk, Nyla Matuk, Shane Neilson, Edward Nixon, Marc di Saverio, and Karen Schindler.

Much appreciation to everyone at Palimpsest Press: particularly Jim Johnstone, Dawn Kresan and Aimee Parent Dunn.

I'm grateful to the Toronto Arts Council and the Ontario Arts Council for financial assistance.

Finally, thank you to my wife, friends, and family for their continued love and support.

Biography

Blair Trewartha is the author of two chapbooks: *Break In* (Cactus Press, 2010) and *Porcupine Burning* (Baseline Press, 2012). His poetry has appeared in *Carousel*, *Contemporary Verse 2*, *Event*, *Existere*, and *Prism International*. Blair grew up in Clinton and has worked as a teacher and writer throughout Ontario. He currently resides in Toronto.